50 STATES TO CELEBRATE

Celebrating
NEW YORK

The text of this book is set in Weidemann.
The display type is set in Bernard Gothic.
The illustrations are drawn with pencil and colored digitally.
The maps are pen, ink, and watercolor.

Photograph of beaver on page 32 © 2013 by Vladimir Chernyanskiy/Alamy
Photograph of bluebird on page 32 © 2013 by iStockphoto.com
Photograph of rose on page 32 © 2013 by Shaughn F. Clements/Alamy

Library of Congress Cataloging-in-Publication Data
Bauer, Marion Dane.
Celebrating New York / by Marion Dane Bauer ; illustrated by C. B. Canga.
p. cm. — (Green light readers level 3) (50 states to celebrate)
ISBN 978-0-547-89781-3 trade paper
ISBN 978-0-547-89782-0 paper over board
1. New York (State)—Juvenile literature. I. Canga, C. B., ill. II. Title.
F119.3.B38 2013
974.7—dc23
2012016878

Manufactured in China
SCP 10 9 8 7 6 5 4 3 2 1
4500394665

50 STATES TO CELEBRATE

Celebrating
NEW YORK

Written by **Marion Dane Bauer**
Illustrated by **C. B. Canga**

sandpiper

Houghton Mifflin Harcourt
Boston   New York   2013

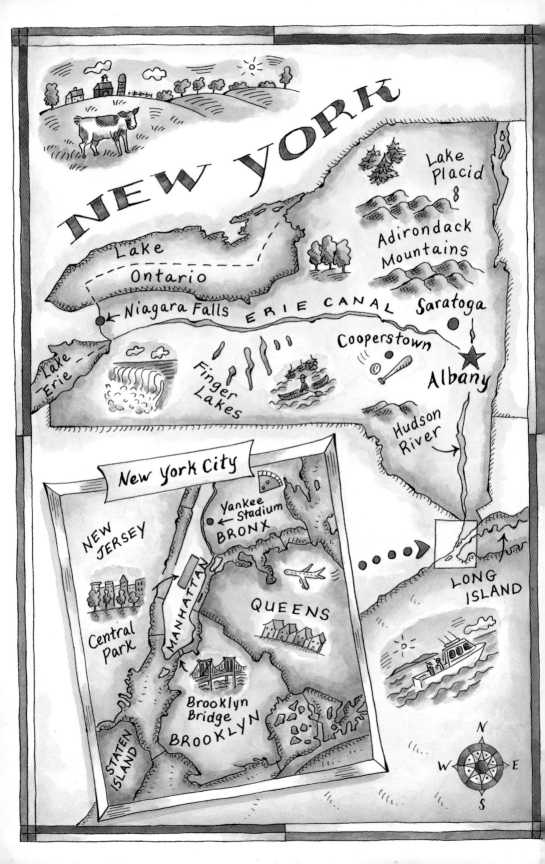

Hi, I'm Mr. Geo.
Can you guess where I am?
I'm visiting the Empire State.
That's right! I'm in New York.

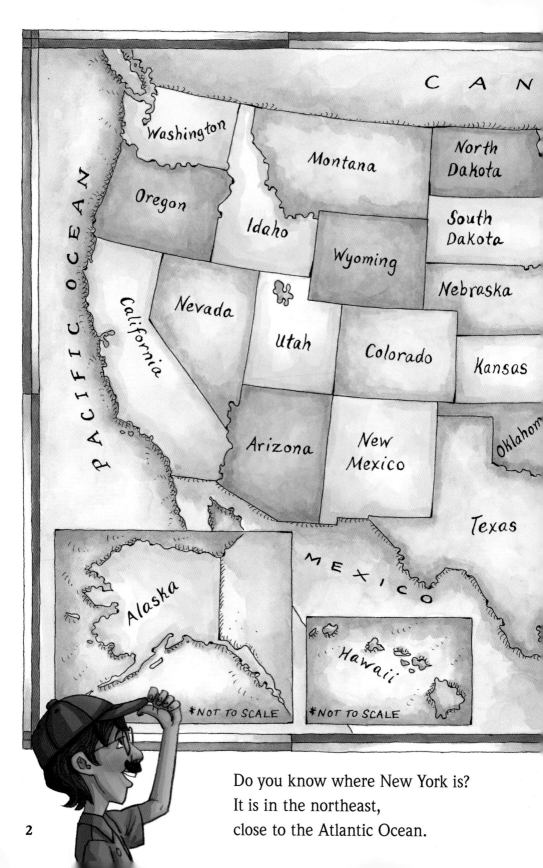

Do you know where New York is?
It is in the northeast,
close to the Atlantic Ocean.

Look north of New Jersey and Pennsylvania.
Then look south of Canada.
There's New York!

3

It's New Year's Eve, and here I am
at Times Square in New York City.
There are thousands of people here with me!
We are all waiting for midnight, when that
shining ball will drop.

Did you know?

New Yorkers have celebrated New Year's Eve by watching a ball drop in Times Square nearly every year since 1907.

Times Square is the center of a world
of theater, dance, and music.
Every night, all along Broadway,
theater after theater lights up
the **Great White Way.**

One block over, the Rockettes kick their way across the stage at Radio City Music Hall. I tried joining the line once, but my feet got in the way!

New York City is often called the Big Apple.

New York City is made up of five main areas,
or **boroughs.**

They are Manhattan, Brooklyn, the Bronx,
Queens, and Staten Island.

Manhattan is the smallest in size,
but it is large in **skyscrapers.**

The Empire State Building was the tallest building
in the world when it opened in 1931.
I like riding the elevator
all the way up to the 86th floor.
The view from here is amazing,
no matter which way I turn!

Central Park lies amid all these skyscrapers.
Its greenery stretches for blocks and blocks.
You can go there to skate, play ball, row a boat,
visit the zoo, or ride a real horse.
But I like the hand-painted horses on the
merry-go-round best!

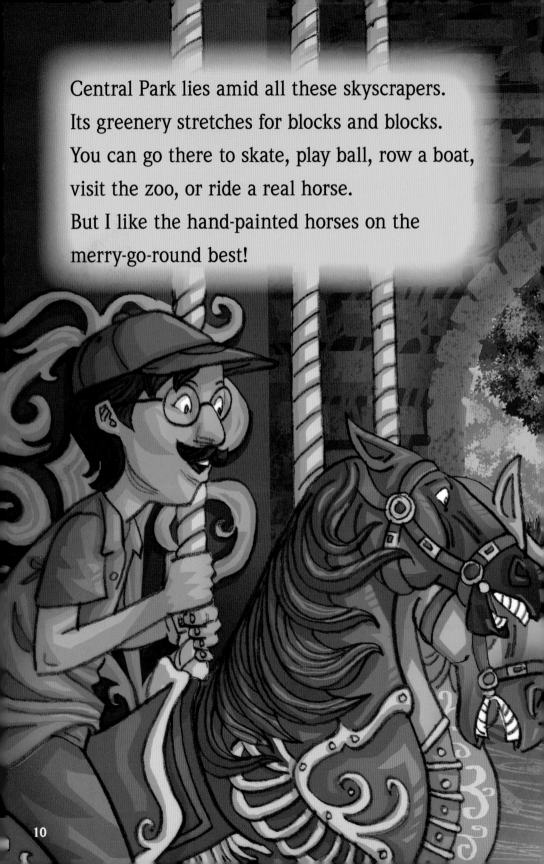

I love to explore the world-famous museums near the park.

Did you know?

At Manhattan's Museum of Natural History you can learn about dinosaurs and outer space!

My favorite place to visit in New York City is
the Statue of Liberty.
She was a gift from France in honor of
our country's 100th birthday.

Millions of **immigrants** from all over the world
have been welcomed to our country by Lady Liberty.
For many years, most of these newcomers
passed through Ellis Island.
They helped to create a city of many **cultures.**

Getting around New York City is easy.
It has the biggest **subway system** in the country.
You can take aboveground trains, buses,
and ferry boats, too.
And, of course, you can drive a car or take a taxi.

But it's a great city for walking!

There are so many people, sights, and stores to see.

All the hustle and bustle makes walking fun!

Did you know?

The Brooklyn Bridge was the first steel-wire **suspension bridge** ever built.

There's more to New York than New York City.
New York is an industrial state and
a farming state and
a state filled with natural wonders.
Care for an apple? Or a glass of milk?
New York farms produce lots of both.

More than half of the state is covered
with forests.
Many birds **migrate** through.
Moose are common in the mountains
to the north.
So are black bears.

Did you know?

New York was the first state to create
state parks by setting aside areas to
be "forever wild."

17

The Yankees and the Mets baseball teams have fans everywhere across the state.
For football, the Jets, the Giants, and the Buffalo Bills call New York home.
New York has three hockey teams, too.

The Yankees slugger Babe Ruth was one of the first players to be chosen for the National Baseball Hall of Fame in Cooperstown, New York.

If you love shooting hoops, as I do, don't forget
the New York Knicks, or the New York Liberty,
a great women's basketball team.
And the Harlem Globetrotters always make
me laugh with their funny tricks!

New York is lucky to have thousands of rivers and streams, lakes, and ponds.

In the summer the water is just right for swimming and sailing.

In the winter I like playing hockey and ice-fishing!

Lake Placid in the Adirondack Mountains hosted the Winter Olympics in 1932 and 1980.

New York even has a manmade **canal.**
The Erie Canal was dug to make travel between
the Hudson River and Lake Erie easier.
People called it a wonder of **engineering** when it
opened in 1825.
Now it's wonderful to bike along the canal.
I don't plan to ride all 365 miles, though!

No water view in New York is more **spectacular** than Niagara Falls!
Three falls stretch between the United States and Canada.

Every minute, millions of gallons of water thunder over **steep** drops.

The highest drop is about 180 feet.

Look out below!

Did you know?

You can put on a raincoat and ride under Niagara Falls on a boat called *Maid of the Mist.*

Here I am in Albany, the capital of New York.
The Dutch set up this area as a fur-trading post
in the early 1600s.
It is one of the oldest cities from the
original 13 **colonies.**

New York played an important part in United States history.
Many of the battles of the **American Revolution** were fought here.

If you visit Saratoga in the fall, you will see people dressed in old-fashioned clothes acting out the Battle of Saratoga from 1777.

But the history of New York began long before
colonial times.
People have lived here for many thousands of years.
The **Iroquois** have been here for about a thousand.

The Iroquois trade routes became some of our paved highways.

Their league of **Five Nations** worked like a **democracy.**

Our country's first leaders may have taken ideas from the Iroquois when they were forming our **government.**

Did you know?

The sport of lacrosse started with Native Americans. The Iroquois have been playing for many years.

There are many heroes in New York history.
Harriet Tubman, Sojourner Truth,
and Horace Greeley fought to end slavery.
Because of these brave people, New York
outlawed slavery in 1827.
That was long before the Civil War ended slavery
in all of the United States.

SOJOURNER
TRUTH

HARRIET
TUBMAN

Elizabeth Cady Stanton, Lucretia Mott, and Susan B. Anthony fought to end slavery too. They also fought for women's rights. A big meeting for women's rights was held in Seneca Falls, New York, in 1848. The activities there led to women gaining the right to vote.

HORACE GREELEY

ELIZABETH CADY STANTON

SUSAN B. ANTHONY

LUCRETIA MOTT

Did you know?

Susan B. Anthony's face is on one type of dollar coin.

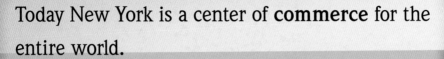

Today New York is a center of **commerce** for the entire world.

And New York City is at the heart of this thriving state.

More than eight million people speaking dozens of different languages live here.

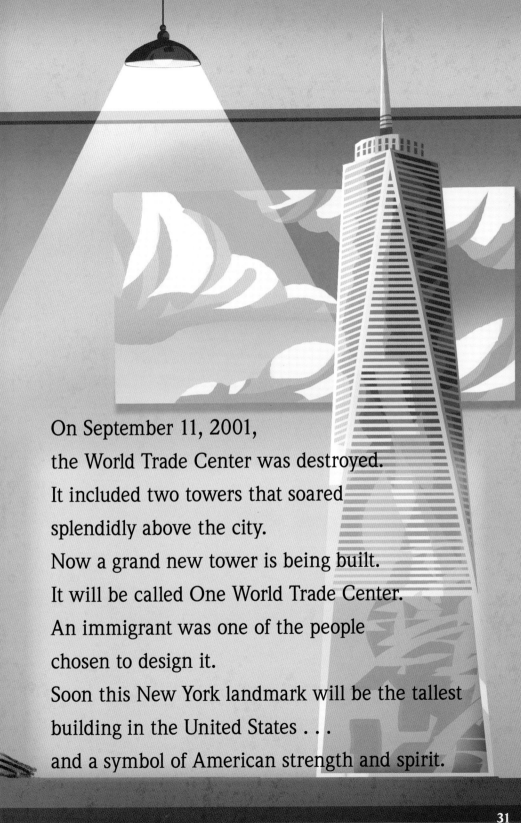

On September 11, 2001,
the World Trade Center was destroyed.
It included two towers that soared
splendidly above the city.
Now a grand new tower is being built.
It will be called One World Trade Center.
An immigrant was one of the people
chosen to design it.
Soon this New York landmark will be the tallest
building in the United States . . .
and a symbol of American strength and spirit.

Fast Facts About New York

Nickname: The Empire State, perhaps because in 1784 George Washington said that New York was "the seat of the empire."

State motto: Ever upward.

State capital: Albany.

Other major cities: Buffalo, New York City, Rochester, Syracuse.

Year of statehood: 1788.

State animal: Beaver.

State bird: Bluebird.

State flower: Rose.

State flag and seal:

Population: Just under 20 million, according to the 2010 U.S. census.

Fun fact: In 1901 New York became the first state to require license plates on automobiles.

Another fun fact: The apple muffin was designated as the official state muffin of New York in 1987.

Dates in New York History

1570: The Iroquois League is formed.

1609: Henry Hudson sails into the Hudson Bay.

1624: Dutch settle the colony they call New Netherland.

1664: British take over the area and rename it New York.

1788: New York becomes the 11th state.

1797: Albany becomes the state capital.

1825: The Erie Canal opens.

1827: Slavery is abolished in New York.

1848: Women gather in Seneca Falls for the first women's rights convention.

1883: The Brooklyn Bridge is completed.

1886: The Statue of Liberty is dedicated.

1931: The Empire State Building is completed.

1952: The United Nations meets in Manhattan for the first time.

2001: The World Trade Center is destroyed.

Activities

1. **LOCATE** the three states on New York's eastern border on the map on pages 2 and 3. Then SAY each state's name out loud.

2. **DESIGN** a picture postcard for New York. On the back, write a short message to a friend about what you drew.

3. **SHARE** two facts you learned about New York with a family member or friend.

4. **PRETEND** you are the governor of New York and a TV travel reporter is going to interview you for a special program on great places to visit. Other governors from other states will be interviewed too. You want to be the best so you do some extra research. If you can answer the following questions correctly, you are sure to be a big hit!

   a. **WHAT** country gave the United States the Statue of Liberty?

   b. **WHERE** is the National Baseball Hall of Fame located?

   c. About **HOW** high is the steepest drop at Niagara Falls?

   d. **WHEN** did the Battle of Saratoga take place?

5. **UNJUMBLE** these words that have something to do with New York. Write your answers on a separate sheet of paper.

   a. **SHTEATRE** (HINT: There are many on Broadway)

   b. **BUWYSA** (HINT: A way to get around New York City)

   c. **PPLEA** (HINT: A fruit)

   d. **SEOOM** (HINT: An animal)

   e. **ESNAYEK** (HINT: A baseball team)

Glossary

American Revolution: the war that won the 13 American colonies freedom from British rule; it took place from 1775–83. (p. 25)

borough: a section of a city or town. (p. 8)

canal: a waterway that is dug to connect bodies of water so ships can move between them. (p. 21)

colony: a settlement ruled by a different country. (p. 24)

commerce: the buying and selling of goods and services. (p. 30)

culture: a way of life shared by a group of people. (p. 13)

democracy: a form of government in which power belongs to the people. (p. 27)

engineering: the use of science to design and build things people need. (p. 21)

Five Nations (also known as the Iroquois League): Five tribes of Native Americans from upstate New York who joined together in the late 1500s; the tribes included the Mohawk, Oneida, Onondaga, Cayuga, and Seneca; the Tuscarora from North Carolina joined the group after 1722 and the league became known as Six Nations. (p. 27)

government: the way a country, city, or town is run; also, the group of people who lead a country, city, or town, including making its laws. (p. 27)

Great White Way: a nickname for the theater district on Broadway in New York City because of all the bright lights at night. (p. 6)

immigrants: people who move to a country from another country. (p. 13)

Iroquois: Native American people from an area in New York. (p. 26)

migrate: to move from one place to another. (p. 17)

skyscrapers: tall buildings. (p. 8)

spectacular: sensational, wonderful. (p. 22)

steep: very high. (p. 23)

subway system: a pathway of railways underground, usually powered by electricity. (p. 14)

suspension bridge: a bridge that is hung from strong cables and supported by towers. (p. 15)

Answers to activities on page 34:

1) Vermont, Massachusetts, and Connecticut; 2) postcards will vary; 3) facts mentioned will vary; 4a) France; 4b) Cooperstown; 4c) about 180 feet; 4d) 1777; 5a) theaters; 5b) subway; 5c) apple; 5d) moose; 5e) Yankees.